MW01206135

WRITERS REPUBLIC

THE HIDDEN SCOURGE OF CHILD SUPPORT ABUSE

BASED ON A TRUE STORY

ANTHONY GOMEZ

Copyright © 2023 by Anthony Gomez.

All rights reserved. No part of this book may be reproduced in any form or by any electronic or mechanical means, including information storage and retrieval systems, without permission in writing from the publisher, except by reviewers, who may quote brief passages in a review.

This publication contains the opinions and ideas of its author. It is intended to provide helpful and informative material on the subjects addressed in the publication. The author and publisher specifically disclaim all responsibility for any liability, loss, or risk, personal or otherwise, which is incurred as a consequence, directly or indirectly, of the use and application of any of the contents of this book.

WRITERS REPUBLIC L.L.C.
515 Summit Ave. Unit R1
Union City, NJ 07087, USA

Website: *www.writersrepublic.com*
Hotline: *1-877-656-6838*
Email: *info@writersrepublic.com*

Ordering Information:
Quantity sales. Special discounts are available on quantity purchases by corporations, associations, and others. For details, contact the publisher at the address above.

Library of Congress Control Number:	2023913508	
ISBN-13:	979-8-88810-970-0	[Paperback Edition]
	979-8-89100-148-0	[Hardback Edition]
	979-8-88810-969-4	[Digital Edition]

Rev. date: 07/20/2023

Unveiling the Hidden Truth: Understanding Child Support from the Perspective of a Victimized Father

In today's society, child support has become an integral part of the legal system, aiming to protect the best interests of children whose parents have separated or divorced. However, amidst the numerous success stories, there exists an often-overlooked narrative of fathers who have been unjustly treated by the system. This book, written from personal experience, aims to shed light on the realities faced by a father who has been bullied by the child support system, challenging the stereotype of the deadbeat father. Through my own struggle, I have gained unique insights into the intricacies of child support, making me qualified to guide and empower others who find themselves in similar circumstances. As the victim of an unjust child support system, I have firsthand knowledge of the challenges and frustrations that fathers face. I have personally experienced the emotional turmoil, financial strain, and legal battles that often accompany this system. My journey has provided me with an intimate understanding of the complexities involved, enabling me to articulate the nuances and difficulties faced by non-custodial parents. Throughout my struggle, I have invested significant time and effort into understanding the legal framework surrounding child support. I have familiarized myself with relevant laws, regulations, and precedents, enabling me to provide accurate information and guidance to others. Additionally, I have conducted extensive research, analyzing case studies, academic literature, and expert opinions to gain a comprehensive understanding of the child support system and its impact on fathers. Driven by my own experiences, I have become an advocate for fathers who have been mistreated by the child support system. I have actively participated in support groups, engaged with legal professionals, and connected with other individuals who have faced similar challenges. Through these interactions, I have developed a network of resources and support that further enhances my ability to provide assistance and guidance to others. As a victim of the system, I understand the emotional toll it can take on individuals. I have experienced the stigma and judgment associated with being labeled a deadbeat father, despite my unwavering commitment to my children's well-being. This empathy and emotional understanding enable me to connect with others who feel trapped or misunderstood, allowing me to provide guidance and encouragement with compassion. My personal journey has equipped me with the necessary qualifications to shed light on the child support system from a perspective often overlooked – that of a victimized father. Through my experiences, legal knowledge, advocacy efforts, and emotional understanding, I am uniquely positioned to empower and guide individuals who find themselves in similar situations. This book aims to expose the flaws and injustices within the child support system while providing practical advice and support to those who need it most. Please Enjoy.

My Dearest Child,

You haven't seen me in years, but I am sitting here writing this letter to you, because I love you, and I think about you every day. I am filled with love and hope for your future. You are the light of my life, my blood, and my soul. Please forgive me. I am so grateful for the joy and happiness you bring into our family. I wanted to take this opportunity to share with you some of the lessons I have learned about love and hope. These are two of the most important things in life, and I hope that you will carry them with you always as you navigate through the ups and downs of life. First, love is a powerful force that can help us overcome any obstacle. It is the foundation of our family and the glue that holds us together. Love is not just a feeling, but an action. It requires us to be patient, kind, and compassionate toward others. Love is also about forgiveness and understanding, and I hope that you will always remember to show love to those around you. Second, hope is what keeps us moving forward even in the darkest of times. It is the belief that things will get better and that we can make a difference in the world. Hope gives us the strength to persevere and to never give up on our dreams. I hope that you will always have hope in your heart, even when things seem difficult. My dear child, I love you more than words can express, and I have so much hope for your future. I believe that you will achieve great things in life, and I will always be here to support and encourage you along the way.

With all my love and hope,
Your Long-Lost Father
PS. We will meet again. Soon.

PREFACE

My book may explore the reasons why some fathers choose to leave their children's lives, particularly in situations where they feel harassed by the system. Because I am a victim, I can only imagine why many fathers leave their children behind. My book may delve into the societal, cultural, and legal factors that contribute to this phenomenon, as well as the emotional toll it takes on both fathers and children. I may also share personal stories and experiences, as well as insights and reflections on how to address this issue. Ultimately, my book may aim to shed light on a complex and often misunderstood topic and to spark a broader conversation about fatherhood, family dynamics, and the challenges of modern parenting. We often hear single mothers picking up the responsibilities after the father leaves, but *why*? We don't ask these questions because we are good at pointing fingers and not digging deeper into the real situations. The mother's outburst out of frustration is "If he only helps me out more" or "Your father doesn't love you" or "Your father is running late again?"

Let's look into the real problems. The children, The communicated system is a resource to pay your responsibility by using the one thing that fathers rely on, which is money. All fathers such as myself fall in this victimized category, "Why Me," when we see forty-hour-a-week checks. As men, we don't have time to cry or feel sorry. As a man, we need to make more money to pay bills. Some work more or pick up a second job neglecting the one person we care about, canceling quality time plans with your children. Let's look inside deeper with data.

INTRODUCTION

According to the US Census Bureau, in 2019, 69% of all children under the age of 18 lived with two parents, while 23% lived with only their mother, 4% lived with only their father, and 4% lived with neither parent.

The National Center for Health Statistics reported that the divorce rate in America is around 39% for first marriages, 60% for second marriages, and 73% for third marriages.

The Pew Research Center found that in 2018, 57% of adults who had been married or lived with a partner said they had ever experienced a major disagreement with their partner about finances, and 29% said money was the biggest source of tension in their relationship.

The Substance Abuse and Mental Health Services Administration reported that in 2019, an estimated 9.4 million adults in the United States had a serious mental illness, and 4.5 million adults had a co-occurring mental illness and substance use disorder, which can strain relationships and contribute to family breakdowns.

The Annie E. Casey Foundation found that children who grow up in single-parent homes are more likely to experience poverty, drop out of school, and have emotional and behavioral problems than children who grow up with two parents. Child support is a legal obligation that a noncustodial parent must pay to the custodial parent for the financial support of their children. Unfortunately, some noncustodial parents abuse this obligation by not paying or underpaying child support. This can have a devastating impact on the children and custodial parents, leading to poverty, homelessness, and a host of other problems.

According to the US Census Bureau, in 2019, 23% of all children under the age of 18 lived with only their mother, while 4% lived with only their father.

The National Fatherhood Initiative reports that children who grow up without a father in the home are four times more likely to live in poverty, seven times more likely to become pregnant as a teen, and more likely to face behavioral problems and have lower academic achievement.

The US Department of Health and Human Services found that children in father-absent homes are at greater risk of suffering from physical, emotional, and sexual abuse and are more likely to engage in drug and alcohol abuse, criminal activity, and other high-risk behaviors.

The Centers for Disease Control and Prevention (CDC) reports that children in father-absent homes are at higher risk of obesity and are more likely to suffer from asthma, mental health problems, and other health issues.

The CDC also reports that children in father-absent homes are more likely to be victims of child abuse and neglect and are more likely to experience adverse childhood experiences that can have lasting effects on their physical and mental health. The family is the basic unit of society, and it plays a crucial role in shaping the lives of individuals. A family is considered broken when the parents are no longer together or when one parent is absent. In this essay, we will focus on the impact of broken families without a father on children and society. According to statistics, the number of broken families has been on the rise in recent years. In the United States, over 50% of marriages end in divorce, and about 40% of children are born to unmarried parents. This means that a significant number of children are growing up without a father figure in their lives. The absence of a father can have a profound impact on children's lives. Children who grow up without a father are more likely to experience poverty, have behavioral problems, and struggle academically. They are

Anthony Gomez

also more likely to engage in risky behaviors such as drug abuse and early sexual activity.

One of the most significant impacts of growing up without a father is poverty. According to the US Census Bureau, children in single-parent households are more likely to live in poverty than those in two-parent households. This is because single-parent households often have lower incomes and fewer resources to provide for their children's needs. Children from broken families without a father are also more likely to have behavioral problems. Studies have shown that children from single-parent households are more likely to exhibit aggressive behavior, have trouble with authority figures, and struggle with emotional regulation. This is because they lack the stability and support that a father figure can provide.

Academically, children from broken families without a father also tend to struggle. According to a study by the National Fatherhood Initiative, children from fatherless homes are more likely to drop out of school, have lower grades, and have lower test scores. This is because they lack the support and guidance that a father can provide in terms of academic achievement. In addition to these challenges, children from broken families without a father are also more likely to engage in risky behaviors. They are more likely to experiment with drugs and alcohol, engage in early sexual activity, and have multiple sexual partners. This is because they lack the guidance and support that a father can provide in terms of making healthy choices.

The impact of growing up without a father is not limited to the individual child. It also has a significant impact on society as a whole. Children who grow up without a father are more likely to become involved in the criminal justice system, and they are more likely to rely on government assistance. According to a study by the National Fatherhood Initiative, children from fatherless homes are more likely to be involved in crime. They are more likely to be incarcerated, and they are more likely to engage in violent behavior. This is because they lack the guidance and support that a father can provide in terms of making positive choices. In addition to the impact on the criminal justice system, children from broken families without a father also tend to rely more on government assistance. According to the US Census Bureau, children in single-parent households are more likely to receive public assistance than those in two-parent households. This is because single-parent households often have lower incomes and fewer resources to provide for their children's needs.

The impact of growing up without a father is not limited to the United States. It is a global issue that affects millions of children around the world. In developing countries, the impact of broken families without a father is even more significant. Children in these countries are more likely to experience poverty, malnutrition, and lack of access to education.

In conclusion, the impact of broken families without a father is significant and far-reaching. Children who grow up without a father are more likely to experience poverty, have behavioral problems, struggle academically, and engage in risky behaviors. They are also more likely to become involved in the criminal justice system and rely on government assistance. The impact of growing up without a father is not only limited to the individual child but also affects society as a whole. It is essential to address this issue and provide support and resources to children from broken families without a father to help them overcome these challenges and lead successful lives.

Anthony Gomez

CHAPTER 1

You Are Not Alone

In this book, we will explore the story of a father who refused to pay child support and the impact it had on his children and their mother. The story begins with a bitter divorce and custody battle between the father, John, and the mother, Sarah. Despite being awarded custody of their two children, Sarah struggled to make ends meet due to John's refusal to pay child support. This led to financial instability and stress for Sarah and her children. John had a variety of excuses for why he couldn't pay child support, including job loss, health problems, and lack of funds. Despite these excuses, he continued to live a comfortable lifestyle and refused to contribute financially to his children's upbringing. The impact of John's refusal to pay child support was devastating for his children. They missed out on opportunities like extracurricular activities and summer camps and struggled with basic needs like food and clothing. They also suffered emotionally, feeling abandoned and unloved by their father. Sarah took legal action to enforce the child support order, but John continued to evade payment. This led to wage garnishment and other enforcement measures, but John still refused to pay. The legal battle was long and exhausting, and Sarah struggled to provide for her children during this time. Despite the challenges they faced, Sarah and her children persevered. Sarah found a better job, and her children excelled in school and extracurricular activities. However, the emotional scars of John's refusal to pay child support remained, and the children struggled to trust their father.

The story of John and Sarah highlights the importance of child support and the devastating impact it can have when it is not paid. It also highlights the need for stronger legal and social responses to child support abuse, as well as the need for greater empathy and understanding from noncustodial parents toward their children and the custodial parent. The story of John and Sarah is just one example of the many families who struggle with child support abuse. By raising awareness of the issue and taking action to address it, we can ensure that all children receive the financial support they need to thrive and succeed.

A Momentous Occasion

The birth of a child is a momentous occasion that is often filled with joy and celebration. But for one father, the arrival of his son brought unexpected emotions and tears that he never anticipated. The story begins with the pregnancy of the father's wife, Maria. The father, named Carlos, was excited and nervous about becoming a father for the first time. He spent months preparing for the arrival of his son, reading parenting books and attending childbirth classes with Maria. When the day finally arrived, Carlos was by Maria's side in the delivery room. As he watched his son being born, he felt a rush of emotions that he didn't expect. He was overwhelmed with love, but also with fear and anxiety about the responsibility of being a father. As Carlos held his son for the first time, he began to cry. At first, he tried to hold back his tears, but they flowed freely and uncontrollably. He felt embarrassed and ashamed for crying, but he couldn't stop. After the birth of his son, Carlos struggled to come to terms with his emotions. He felt like he had failed as a father by crying and showing vulnerability. He tried to hide his tears from his wife and family, but they could see that he was struggling. As time passed, Carlos came to realize that his tears were not a sign of weakness, but a sign of love and devotion to his son. He began to embrace his emotions and show his son and family the depth of his love and commitment. The story of Carlos and his tears highlights the importance of embracing emotions and vulnerability, especially in the context of fatherhood. It also underscores the need for fathers to be present and engaged in the lives of their children and to show their love and commitment in tangible ways. The tears of a father are a powerful expression of love and devotion to his children. By embracing our emotions and vulnerability, we can become better fathers and role models for our children.

Tom had a child with his ex-girlfriend Sarah. After their relationship ended, Sarah had full custody of their son, and Tom was ordered by the court to pay child support. At first, Tom was hesitant about paying child support. He had always been skeptical about the system and had heard horror stories from his friends about how much money they had to pay. However, after a few months of avoiding the issue, Tom finally decided to face it head-on. He went to the courthouse and asked to see his child support check. When he saw the amount, he was shocked. It was much lower than he had anticipated. Tom had been worried that he wouldn't be able to make ends meet, but the amount he had to pay was manageable. Tom realized that he had been avoiding his responsibility as a father. He had been so focused on the negative aspects of child support that he had forgotten about the positive aspects. He had a son who needed his support, and he was finally able to provide it. Tom started paying his child support regularly and began to build a relationship with his son. He would take him out for ice cream, play catch with him, and help him with his homework. Tom realized that being a father was not just about providing financial support; it was about being there for his child in every way possible. Over time, Tom's relationship with his ex-girlfriend also improved. They were able to communicate better and work together for the benefit of their son. Tom even started to appreciate the court system that had helped him become a responsible father. In the end, Tom realized that paying child support was not a burden but a privilege. He was grateful for the opportunity to be a father to his son and to provide him with the support he needed. And most importantly, he learned that being a good father was about love, commitment, and responsibility, not just money.

John had always been a hardworking man. He had a good job and a loving family. He had been married to his wife, Mary, for ten years; and they had a beautiful daughter, Sarah. John loved them both more than anything in the world. But one day, everything changed. John lost his job due to the company's downsizing. He searched for a new job, but it seemed that no one was hiring. Bills started piling up, and he was struggling to make ends meet. To make matters worse, John received a notice from the child support agency that he was behind on his payments. He knew he owed money, but he didn't have any extra cash to spare. He had been sending what he could, but it wasn't enough. The agency took his last dollar, leaving him with nothing. John was devastated. He didn't know what to do. He couldn't even afford to buy groceries for his family. Mary tried to be supportive, but she was worried about how they were going to survive. John felt like a failure. He couldn't provide for his family anymore. He spent his days looking for a new job, but it seemed like no one wanted to hire him. He felt hopeless and depressed. One day, Sarah came to him and asked why he was always sad. John didn't know how to explain it to her, so he just hugged her tightly. He realized that he needed to be strong for his family. He needed to find a way to provide for them.

John started looking for odd jobs around the neighborhood. He mowed lawns, cleaned gutters, and did whatever he could to earn some money. It wasn't much, but it was enough to buy groceries and pay some bills. Slowly but surely, John started to get back on his feet. He found a new job and was able to catch up on his child support payments. He realized that even though life can be tough, he had to keep fighting for his family. John learned that no matter how hard things get, he could never give up. He knew he had to be strong for his family, and that's exactly what he did.

James was a single father who had recently lost his job. He had a young son named Michael, whom he loved more than anything in the world. James had been struggling to make ends meet, but he always managed to put food on the table for Michael. One day, James realized that he didn't have any money left to buy food. He had been behind on his bills and had used up all his savings. He didn't know what to do. He didn't want his son to go hungry. James decided to take Michael to a local soup kitchen to get some food. He was embarrassed, but he knew it was the only way to feed his son. Michael didn't understand what was going on, but he was happy to be spending time with his dad. As they were leaving the soup kitchen, James saw his ex-wife, Sarah, walking toward them. He hadn't seen her in months. Sarah had left him and Michael when Michael was just a baby. She had moved to another state and hadn't been in touch since. Sarah saw James and Michael and stopped in her tracks. She couldn't believe how much Michael had grown. She asked James what he was doing at the soup kitchen. James explained that he had lost his job and didn't have any money to feed Michael. Sarah was shocked. She had no idea that James was struggling. She offered to help, but James refused. He didn't want to take anything from her. Sarah insisted and gave him some money to buy food. A few days later, James received a notice from the child support agency. Sarah had filed a claim against him, saying that he hadn't been paying child support. James was devastated. He had been doing everything he could to take care of Michael, but he knew he was behind on his payments. James went to court to fight the claim, but he didn't have any proof that he had been trying to pay. Sarah had all the evidence she needed to support her claim. James was ordered to pay a large sum of money that he didn't have.

James felt like he had failed as a father. He couldn't provide for his son, and now he was in debt. He didn't know how he was going to pay the money back. He was worried that he would lose Michael.

But James didn't give up. He found a new job and started making payments toward his debt. He knew it was going to be a long road, but he was determined to provide for his son. He realized that even though life can be tough, he had to keep fighting for his family.

David had always been a hardworking man. He had a good job and a loving family. He had been divorced from his wife, Sarah, for a few years; but he still loved his two children more than anything in the world. David had been paying child support to Sarah every month, but he had noticed that his payments had been increasing without any explanation. He had been struggling to make ends meet, but he always managed to send the money to Sarah. One day, David received his paycheck and noticed that the entire amount had been taken by the child support agency. He didn't understand why. He had been sending his payments on time and in full. David called the agency, but he couldn't get a straight answer. He was told that he owed more money than he had been sending and that he needed to pay the full amount immediately. David didn't have any extra cash to spare. He had bills to pay and a family to feed. David felt like he had been betrayed. He had always done his best to provide for his children, but now he couldn't even afford to put food on the table. He decided to quit his job, knowing that he wouldn't be able to support his family with the child support payments taking his entire paycheck.

David's decision to quit his job was met with anger from Sarah. She accused him of being a deadbeat dad and not caring about his children. David tried to explain his situation, but Sarah wouldn't listen. David spent the next few months looking for a new job. He sent out countless resumes and went on countless interviews, but he couldn't find anything. Bills started piling up, and he was struggling to make ends meet. David realized that he couldn't give up. He had to find a way to provide for his family. He started doing odd jobs around the neighborhood, anything to earn some money. It wasn't much, but it was enough to buy groceries and pay some bills. Slowly but surely, David started to get back on his feet. He found a new job and was able to catch up on his child support payments. He realized that even though life can be tough, he had to keep fighting for his family. David learned that no matter how hard things get, he could never give up. He knew he had to be strong for his family, and that's exactly what he did.

Single Development

Being single can be both liberating and challenging. It can be a time for self-discovery, personal growth, and independence. However, it can also be a time of loneliness, longing for companionship, and societal pressure to find a partner. For some, being single is a choice, while for others, it may be a result of circumstances such as a breakup, divorce, or simply not finding the right person yet. Regardless of the reason, single life can offer many opportunities for personal development. One of the most significant advantages of being single is the freedom to pursue one's passions and interests without the need to compromise with a partner. Single individuals can focus on their careers, hobbies, and personal goals without feeling guilty or obligated to prioritize their partner's needs. This can lead to a sense of fulfillment and satisfaction in one's personal achievements.

Single life also allows for the opportunity to build meaningful friendships and connections. Without a partner, individuals may seek out social activities and events that align with their interests, leading to new friendships and potential romantic relationships. Additionally, single individuals may have more time and energy to invest in existing friendships and family relationships, strengthening those bonds. On the other hand, being single can also be challenging. One of the most significant difficulties is the feeling of loneliness and isolation. Single individuals may feel left out of social events or may struggle to find meaningful connections with others. This can lead to feelings of depression and anxiety, which can be detrimental to one's mental health. Another challenge of single life is the societal pressure to find a partner. Society often places a high value on romantic relationships, and single individuals may feel like they are not meeting societal expectations. This can lead to feelings of inadequacy, low self-esteem, and a sense of failure. Despite the challenges, being single can be an empowering and fulfilling experience. With the right mindset and support system, single individuals can navigate the ups and downs of single life and come out stronger and more self-aware.

One of the most significant benefits of being single is the opportunity for self-discovery. Single individuals have the freedom to explore their own values, beliefs, and desires without the influence of a partner. This can lead to a deeper sense of self-awareness and personal growth. Additionally, single individuals have the opportunity to develop a strong sense of independence. Without a partner, single individuals must learn to rely on themselves and be self-sufficient. This can lead to a sense of confidence and empowerment that can be beneficial in all areas of life. Single life also allows for the opportunity to travel and explore the world. Without the need to consider a partner's schedule or preferences, single individuals can plan trips and adventures that align with their own interests and desires. This can lead to new experiences, cultural immersion, and personal growth. Despite the benefits of being single, many individuals still long for companionship and romantic love. While being single can be fulfilling, there is no denying the benefits of a healthy and loving relationship. However, it is important to remember that a relationship should enhance one's life, not define it. Single individuals should take the time to focus on their personal growth and self-discovery, and trust that the right partner will come along when the time is right.

In conclusion, being single can be both liberating and challenging. It not only offers the opportunity for personal growth, self-discovery, and independence, but also comes with the challenges of loneliness and societal pressure. With the right mindset, support system, and sense of self-awareness, single individuals can navigate the ups and downs of single life and come out stronger and more fulfilled.

However, I can provide an objective perspective on the issue of fathers who haven't seen their children because of child support because I am a father who's going through this situation along with millions of fathers. Child support is a legal obligation that a noncustodial parent, often the father, is required to pay to the custodial parent, usually the mother, to support their children's basic needs and expenses. Child support is usually determined by the court based on the noncustodial parent's income, the number of children, and other factors. Failure to pay child support can result in legal consequences such as wage garnishment, license suspension, and even imprisonment. While child support is intended to ensure that children receive the financial support they need, it can also have unintended consequences, particularly for fathers who are unable to pay or who feel that they are being unfairly treated. One of the most significant consequences of child support is that it can lead to fathers being unable to see their children. Some fathers may feel that they are being punished for their inability to pay child support, while others may be denied access to their children as a result of disputes with the custodial parent or other factors. In some cases, fathers may choose to avoid paying child support altogether, believing that they are being unfairly targeted or that the amount they are required to pay is excessive. This can lead to legal consequences and further exacerbate the situation. However, it is important to note that there are also many cases in which fathers are genuinely unable to pay child support due to financial hardship or other factors. In these cases, it may be necessary to seek legal assistance or other forms of support to address the issue. Regardless of the reasons behind a father's inability to pay child support, it is important to recognize the impact that this can have on both the father and the child.

Children who are denied access to their fathers may experience emotional and psychological distress, while fathers who are unable to see their children may also suffer from depression, anxiety, and other mental health issues. In addition to the emotional toll, the financial burden of child support can also have a significant impact on fathers.

Many fathers may struggle to make ends meet while paying child support, particularly if they are also responsible for other expenses such as rent, utilities, and food. Furthermore, the legal consequences of failing to pay child support can further exacerbate these financial difficulties, leading to wage garnishment, license suspension, and other penalties that can make it even more challenging for fathers to meet their financial obligations. Ultimately, the issue of fathers who haven't seen their children because of child support is a complex and multifaceted one. While child support is necessary to ensure that children receive the financial support they need, it is important to consider the impact that this can have on fathers and to work toward solutions that are fair and equitable for all parties involved. One potential solution is to provide greater support and resources for fathers who are struggling to meet their child support obligations. This could include financial assistance, job training and placement, and other forms of support that can help fathers to meet their financial obligations and maintain a relationship with their children. Another solution is to work toward a more equitable system of child support that takes into account the unique circumstances of each family. This could involve more flexible payment plans, adjustments based on changes in income, and other measures that can help to ensure that child support is fair and reasonable for all parties involved. Ultimately, the most important thing is to recognize the importance of fathers in the lives of their children and to work toward solutions that support the well-being of both fathers and children. By addressing the issue of fathers who haven't seen their children because of child support in a compassionate and equitable way, we can help to ensure that all children have access to the love and support of both parents, regardless of their financial circumstances.

Mothers Accountable for Misusing the Money

Mothers who do not use child support money for their children are a growing concern in society. Child support is a legal obligation that a noncustodial parent must pay to the custodial parent to assist with the financial needs of the child. However, some mothers misuse the money or spend it on themselves, instead of using it for the children's needs. One of the most common reasons why mothers do not use the child support money for their children is due to financial mismanagement. They may be struggling with their own finances, and the child support money may be used to pay off their debts or bills. This can leave the children without the necessary resources they need, such as food, clothing, or school supplies. Another reason why mothers do not use the child support money for their children is due to substance abuse issues. They may be addicted to drugs or alcohol, and the money may be used to fuel their addiction instead of being used for the children's needs. This can lead to neglect and abuse of the children, which is unacceptable. Moreover, some mothers may use the child support money for their own personal gain, such as buying luxury items or going on vacations. This is a clear violation of the court order, and it can lead to legal consequences.

It is important to note that not all mothers misuse the child support money. Many mothers use it as intended, to provide for their children's needs and ensure their well-being. However, for those who do misuse the money, it is crucial to hold them accountable for their actions. Enforcing child support orders and holding mothers accountable for misusing the money can help ensure that children receive the financial support they need. It is also important to provide education and resources to help mothers manage their finances and overcome substance abuse issues so they can provide for their children's needs.

In conclusion, mothers who do not use the child support money for their children are a growing concern in our society. It is crucial to hold them accountable for their actions and provide resources to help them manage their finances and overcome substance abuse issues. Ultimately, the well-being of the children should be the top priority.

Can mothers get into trouble if they are not using child support money for their children?

(Ask your family attorney about this matter.)

Disclaimer: I *am not* playing the role of attorney nor am I practicing.

The short answer is yes, mothers can get into trouble if they are not using child support money for their children. Child support is a legal obligation that a noncustodial parent must pay to the custodial parent to assist with the financial needs of the child. The money is intended to provide for the child's basic needs, such as food, clothing, and shelter. If a mother is not using the money for its intended purpose, she may face legal consequences. One of the main consequences of misusing child support money is that the custodial parent can take legal action against the noncustodial parent. This can include taking them to court to enforce the child support order or seeking a modification of the order if the noncustodial parent is not meeting their financial obligations. The custodial parent can also report the noncustodial parent to the state agency responsible for enforcing child support orders. If a mother is found to be misusing child support money, she may face legal consequences as well. Depending on the severity of the offense, she may be charged with contempt of court or fraud. Contempt of court occurs when a person violates a court order, such as using child support money for personal expenses instead of the child's needs. Fraud occurs when a person intentionally deceives another person for personal gain, such as using child support money for luxury items or vacations.

In addition to legal consequences, a mother who misuses child support money may also face social consequences. Friends and family members may view her actions as selfish or irresponsible, and she may lose their support. The child may also suffer emotional and psychological harm if they do not receive the financial support they need. It is important to note that not all cases of misusing child support money are intentional. Some mothers may struggle with financial management or have difficulty prioritizing their child's needs. In these cases, it may be helpful for the mother to seek financial counseling or other resources to help her manage her finances and provide for her child's needs.

In conclusion, mothers can get into trouble if they are not using child support money for their children. The consequences can include legal action, social consequences, and emotional harm to the child. It is important for mothers to prioritize their child's needs and use child support money for its intended purpose. If a mother is struggling with financial management, she may benefit from seeking resources and support to help her provide for her child's needs.

The Provider

The concept of a man being a provider has been deeply ingrained in society for centuries. Men are expected to be the primary breadwinners and financial supporters of their families. This expectation has been perpetuated through various cultural and societal norms, including gender roles and expectations placed on men from a young age. From a young age, boys are taught to be strong, independent, and self-sufficient. They are encouraged to pursue careers that will provide them with financial stability and the ability to support themselves and their families. This emphasis on financial success and stability is reinforced by the media, where successful men are often portrayed as wealthy and powerful.

As boys grow into men, the pressure to provide for their families only increases. Men are expected to be the primary earners in their households, and failure to do so can result in feelings of inadequacy and shame. This can lead to a cycle of stress and anxiety, as men feel the need to constantly provide for their families and maintain their status as providers. Despite the societal pressure to be a provider, there are many men who struggle with this role. Financial instability, unemployment, and other factors can make it difficult for men to fulfill this expectation. This can lead to feelings of shame and failure, as men struggle to meet the expectations placed upon them. However, it is important to note that the concept of a man being a provider is not inherently negative. Providing for one's family can be a source of pride and fulfillment, as men are able to support their loved ones and provide them with a comfortable life. It is only when this expectation becomes a burden that it becomes problematic. In addition to societal pressure, there are also biological and evolutionary factors that may contribute to male reasoning when it comes to being a provider. Throughout history, men have been the primary hunters and gatherers, responsible for providing food and resources for their families. This biological imperative may contribute to the sense of responsibility that men feel when it comes to providing for their loved ones.

Furthermore, there is evidence to suggest that men are more likely to be motivated by financial success and status than women. This may be due to societal conditioning, but it may also be rooted in biology. Studies have shown that men have higher levels of testosterone, which is associated with ambition and competitiveness. This may contribute to the drive that many men feel to succeed financially and provide for their families. However, it is important to note that not all men feel this pressure to be providers. There are many men who reject traditional gender roles and strive for more egalitarian relationships with their partners. These men may prioritize emotional support and connection over financial success and may view their role in the family as equal to their partner's. Ultimately, the concept of male reasoning when it comes to being a provider is complex and multifaceted. While societal pressure and biological factors may contribute to this expectation, it is important to recognize that not all men feel the need to fulfill this role. Furthermore, it is important to acknowledge that the pressure to be a provider can be harmful, leading to feelings of inadequacy and shame. By challenging traditional gender roles and embracing more egalitarian relationships, we can create a society that values emotional support and connection over financial success. So why do males fall behind when the system takes away our ability as a provider? Because we just want to provide—that's in our blood to be the breadwinner for our family.

CHAPTER 2

My Story

Business Trip

It was the year 2020, and the world was hit by a pandemic that no one saw coming. The world was in chaos, and everyone was struggling to survive. I was no exception. Donald Trump announced to the nation about a deadly germ. "Stay home and be safe." At that very moment over the dinner table, I told my wife I was opening a business. She replied, "The nation is down and all you can think about is opening a business, and your job? What?" She looked angry. "I'm seeing someone, and I want a divorce." I realized my marriage just ended. We were two completely different people. As I was explaining my business plans to her, she said, "Stop thinking of yourself and think about your kids for once. Who's going to pay for the kids' insurance if you quit your job? Stop!"

"Okay then," I replied. Statistics reported that the divorce rate in America is around 39% for first marriages. I was part of this statistics. Never thought in a million years I would be a middle-aged father only seeing my kids in the hands of the court schedules. Yes, my marriage ended, but this doesn't mean I am a deadbeat father. I am a father who is going to tell you my story about the child support system. I decided to jump for it and open my business because I was tired of waiting to jump. The time is now. We were in the bedroom, and my oldest son overheard me say, "I am tired of providing for this family." A crack door sounded as it opened.

My son said, "Daddy, are you leaving us?" Getting ready to leave for a long "business trip" I couldn't help but feel a heavy heart. My son, who was only six years old, stood by the window, watching me intently. I knew he was upset about me leaving, but I didn't realize just how much until I saw tears streaming down his face. I walked over to him and knelt down, wrapping my arms around him.

"Hey, buddy, what's wrong?" I asked, trying to hold back my own tears.

"I don't want you to go, Daddy," he sobbed. "I'll miss you so much." I felt a lump in my throat as I held him close. I had always known that leaving my family for work trips was hard on them, but seeing my son cry like this made it even more difficult.

"I know it's tough, buddy," I said, wiping away his tears. "But I promise I'll come back soon. And while I'm gone, you can call me anytime you want. We can talk about anything you want, okay?" He nodded, still sniffling. I knew it would take some time for him to adjust to me being gone, but I hoped that staying connected through phone calls and video chats would help ease the pain. As I hugged him one last time before leaving, I couldn't help but feel grateful for the love and bond I shared with my son. Even though it was hard to leave him behind, I knew that our connection would always be strong, no matter how far apart we were. Staring at the rear mirror and him crying for me was the worst day of my life, and just like that, I was gone. It was the year 2020, and the world was hit by a pandemic that no one saw coming. The world was in chaos, and everyone was struggling to survive. I was no exception. I lost my job, my kids, and my wife. I was kicked out of my apartment, and I had nowhere to go. I was homeless, living on the streets with just a camera and little hope. I was a photographer, and I used to take pictures of beautiful landscapes and people. But now, my camera was my only possession, and it was all I had left.

Every day, I would roam the streets with my camera, taking pictures of the empty roads and deserted buildings. I would capture the sadness and despair of the people who were struggling to survive. I would often sleep on my pickup truck back seat, with nothing to cover myself but my camera gears. Days turned into weeks, and weeks turned into months. I was losing hope, and I felt like giving up. But then something unexpected happened. One day, as I was filming in the city, a woman approached me. She was a wedding photographer. She asked me if she could take my picture and interview me. I agreed, and she was still booking a wedding during this tough time. I told her if I can go with her to a wedding to do a video and show it to her client for free. She was delighted that I offered, and it caught the attention of a few people at the wedding party. They were moved by my story, and they offered to help spread the word for me, then the rest was history. With their help, I was able to get back on my feet. I got a job as a wedding videographer for a local area, and I was able to rent a small apartment. My life changed, and I realized that there is always hope, even in the darkest of times. My camera, which was once my only possession, became my ticket to a better life. It'd been months, and I hadn't heard from my boys. I wondered if they were okay. The nation was still shut down, and everyone was enjoying time with their families.

As I sat on the couch, drunk staring at the TV screen, tears streamed down my face. I thought, *Am I really a deadbeat father?* I was drunk wearing my boxers, holding a beer. I was watching old home videos of myself and my family. Memories flooded my mind, and a deep sense of sadness consumed me. I took my kids to Walt Disney last year. Why did they call me a deadbeat father? I asked myself while I took a drink. Why me? Why this? Why now, during this stupid pandemic? I can't even go to a bar and meet people. Everyone was home with their loved ones while I had a beer in my hands, watching home videos. I saw myself as a child, running around in the backyard with my siblings, laughing and playing without a care in the world. My parents were there too, smiling and enjoying the moment. It was a simpler time, a time when life was easy and carefree. But as I watched more videos, I saw the changes that came with time. My siblings grew up and moved away. My parents aged and became more distant. I saw myself struggling with school, relationships, and life in general. The videos reminded me of all the things I had lost, all the people who had left me, and all the dreams that had faded away. I felt like a failure, like I had let down everyone who had ever believed in me. The more I watched, the more depressed I became. I couldn't stop the tears from flowing, and I couldn't shake the feeling of loneliness that had taken hold of me.

But then something changed. As I watched the videos of myself as a young child, I saw a glimmer of hope. I saw the innocence and joy that I had once possessed, and I realized that it was still within me. I made a decision to stop dwelling on the past and start living in the present. I picked up the phone and called my siblings, my parents, and my friends. I reached out to people I had lost touch with and made plans to reconnect. I realized that life is not about the things we have lost, but about the things we still have. It's about the people who love us, the memories we have made, and the moments we have yet to experience. As I turned off the TV and wiped away my tears, I felt a sense of peace wash over me. I knew that the road ahead would not be easy, but I was ready to face it with a renewed sense of hope and purpose. I tried to distract myself by scrolling through my phone, but the emptiness inside of me only grew stronger. Finally, I reached for a napkin and a pen and began to write down my feelings. "I feel so alone," I wrote, my handwriting shaky and uneven. "I don't have anyone to talk to or to share my life with. It's like I'm invisible to everyone around me." As I continued to write, the words poured out of me like a waterfall. I wrote about my fears, my doubts, and my insecurities. I wrote about how it felt to be surrounded by people but still feel so isolated. The napkin quickly filled up with my thoughts and emotions, and I felt a sense of relief wash over me. For the first time in a long time, I was acknowledging my feelings instead of pushing them away. As I read over what I had written, I realized that I didn't have to feel this way forever. I could take steps to change my situation, to reach out to others and build meaningful connections. I folded the napkin and tucked it into my pocket, a reminder that I was not alone and that there was always hope for a brighter future.

CHAPTER 3
My Luck Is Over

Three months later, I got a letter from the attorney general's office stating that I have an appointment with the attorney general caseworker who was dealing with my case. She sat down and asked me uncomfortable questions like why did I leave my family? I replied with a smile that I didn't leave my family. I was on a business trip. She asked me, "Can you keep a job for more than twelve months? We are going to get your money and get you with late fees. Do you realize I have the power to take your car, your job, your house, everything?"

I smiled quietly. I told her, "Ma'am, with all due respect, I have a business that is in the process of making six figures this year. And you will have my attorney speak to you." Without any hesitation, she smiled and handed me my papers politely. That evening, I got a call from the attorney general's office. It was a young lady who had a low voice. She was the department director manager who helped fathers look for a minimum-wage job to pay child support. She told me she couldn't find me on the work system, so they had me down as a high-risk case and a red flag. I told her, "Ma'am, what is that high risk of what?" She couldn't give me more information. All she said is the red flag of taking all wages in your earnings report. Without a court hearing, I already dealt with two different workers who judged me without hearing my side. It was a negative experience that blew my mind and made me feel like a deadbeat father. The next morning, I was on the hunt for the best attorney in town, the one who will fight for me and give me a chance to fight for my kids. I had talked to family attorneys about my situation with my soon-to-be ex-wife. My marriage ended but not my responsibility as a father. That attorney had great reviews with past clients in town.

I was at the attorney's office, waiting for my faith. The attorney said, "Please have a seat." I sat down, looking around. The attorney asked, "Why did you come here?"

I replied to find certainty and a moment of clarity. I handed him my paperwork. He smiled and said, "When do you want to start?"

Risk a Lengthy Court Battle

As I sat across from my divorce attorney, I couldn't help but feel a sense of disappointment. I had hired him to fight for me, to protect my rights and ensure that I received a fair settlement in my divorce. But as we went over the details of my case, it became clear that he wasn't going to be the advocate I had hoped for. Throughout the divorce process, I had felt like I was constantly fighting an uphill battle. My ex-wife had a female lawyer who was aggressive and unyielding, and I knew that I needed someone to stand up to her. That's why I had hired my attorney, hoping that he would be the voice I needed in the courtroom. But as we discussed the various aspects of my case, my attorney seemed more interested in settling than in fighting. He kept telling me that it was better to compromise than to risk a lengthy court battle, and I couldn't help but feel like he was giving up too easily. I wanted someone who would fight tooth and nail for me, who would be willing to take on my ex-wife's female attorney and not back down until I got what I was entitled to. I was new with this matter. I didn't know better. We were focusing more on the money than the real case of this. I filmed a wedding, so I know the true value of marriage and what it means to be in a covenant when two people unite together. We broke that covenant with legal obligations.

As the months went by, I watched as my ex-wife's lawyer made aggressive moves, filing motions and dragging out the proceedings. Meanwhile, my attorney remained passive, content to let things play out without putting up much of a fight. I began to feel like I was being taken advantage of, like I was being pushed around by a system that didn't care about my needs. In the end, the settlement I received was far from what I had hoped for. I felt like I had been shortchanged, like I had been forced to settle for less than I deserved. And as I walked out of the courtroom, I couldn't help but feel like my attorney had let me down. I lost everything, even my rights as a father. I remember looking up with anger telling myself why me. It was then that I knew I had to take matters into my own hands. I began researching divorce law, studying the ins and outs of the legal system, and learning everything I could about how to fight for my rights. And as I did so, I realized that there were countless other men out there who were going through the same struggles that I had faced. I wasn't the only father going through this. That's why I decided to write a book about my experiences, to share my story with others who were going through the same thing. I wanted to provide a road map for fathers who were struggling to navigate the legal system, to give broken families the tools they needed to have a relationship with their child after the war.

As I sat down to write, I found that the words flowed easily. I poured out my heart and soul onto the page, recounting every detail of my struggle and sharing the hard-won lessons I had learned along the way. And as I wrote, I felt a sense of empowerment, knowing that my story could help others find the strength to fight for their own rights. In the end, my divorce attorney may not have fought for me, but I refused to let that be the end of my story. Instead, I used my experience to fuel a new passion, to become an advocate for fathers who were struggling to find their own voice in the legal system. And as I look back on my journey, I realize that sometimes the greatest victories come not from winning in court, but from finding the strength to stand up for yourself and fight for what's right: your children's love.

CHAPTER 4
Justice and Rights

Justice and rights are two fundamental concepts that are essential for creating a fair and equitable society. Justice refers to the idea of fairness, where everyone is treated equally, and their rights are protected. Rights, on the other hand, are the entitlements that individuals possess by virtue of being human beings. These entitlements include civil, political, social, and economic rights that are necessary for individuals to live a fulfilling life. The concept of justice has been debated for centuries, and there are many different theories and perspectives on what constitutes justice. One of the most influential theories of justice is that of John Rawls, who argued that justice is achieved when everyone has an equal opportunity to achieve their goals and aspirations. This idea is based on the principle of fairness, where everyone is treated equally, and their rights are protected. The idea of rights is also an essential component of justice. Rights are the entitlements that individuals possess by virtue of being human beings. These entitlements include civil, political, social, and economic rights that are necessary for individuals to live a fulfilling life. Civil rights include the right to freedom of speech, religion, and assembly. Political rights include the right to vote and participate in the political process. Social rights include the right to education, health care, and housing. Economic rights include the right to work and receive fair wages.

The concept of justice and rights is closely linked to the idea of equality. Equality is the idea that everyone should be treated equally, regardless of their race, gender, religion, or social status. This idea is essential for creating a fair and equitable society, where everyone has the opportunity to succeed. However, achieving justice and protecting rights is not always easy. There are many obstacles that can prevent individuals from accessing their rights and achieving justice. Discrimination, poverty, and inequality are just a few of the barriers that can prevent individuals from accessing their rights and achieving justice. Discrimination is a significant obstacle to achieving justice and protecting rights. Discrimination can take many forms, including racial discrimination, gender discrimination, and discrimination based on sexual orientation. Discrimination can prevent individuals from accessing their rights and achieving justice, as it can limit their opportunities and prevent them from participating in society. Poverty is another significant obstacle to achieving justice and protecting rights. Poverty can prevent individuals from accessing their basic needs, such as food, shelter, and health care. It can also limit their opportunities and prevent them from participating in society. Poverty can also perpetuate inequality, as those who are born into poverty often have fewer opportunities and fewer resources to achieve their goals. Inequality is another significant obstacle to achieving justice and protecting rights. Inequality can take many forms, including income inequality, wealth inequality, and social inequality. Inequality can limit individuals' opportunities and prevent them from accessing their rights. It can also perpetuate discrimination and poverty, as those who are born into disadvantaged groups often face more significant obstacles to achieving their goals. To achieve justice and protect rights, it is essential to address these obstacles and create a fair and equitable society. This can be done through various means, such as education, social programs, and policy changes.

Education is one way to address these obstacles and promote justice and rights. Education can provide individuals with the knowledge and skills they need to achieve their goals and participate in society. It can also promote equality and reduce discrimination and inequality. Social programs are another way to address these obstacles and promote justice and rights. Social programs can provide individuals with the resources they need to access their basic needs and achieve their goals. They can also promote equality and reduce poverty and inequality. Policy changes are also essential for achieving justice and protecting rights. Policy changes can address systemic issues that prevent individuals from accessing their rights and achieving justice. They can also promote equality and reduce discrimination and inequality.

In conclusion, justice and rights are essential concepts that are necessary for creating a fair and equitable society. Achieving justice and protecting rights requires addressing obstacles such as discrimination, poverty, and inequality. By promoting education, social programs, and policy changes, we can create a society where everyone has an equal opportunity to achieve their goals and aspirations.

Challenging Task

Starting a business is a challenging task, and it becomes even more challenging when you have no family support. It can be demotivating and discouraging when the people closest to you don't believe in your vision and goals. However, it's essential to remember that you don't need anyone's permission or support to start a business. It's your dream, and you have to take responsibility for making it happen. You have to believe in yourself and your abilities. Starting a business with no family support means that you have to be resourceful and creative. You have to find alternative ways to finance your business, such as applying for loans or grants. You also have to network with other entrepreneurs and build relationships with potential investors. Moreover, it's crucial to surround yourself with people who believe in you and your vision. Seek out mentors and advisors who can guide you through the process of starting and growing your business. Join business associations and attend networking events to meet like-minded individuals who can offer support and advice. Starting a business with no family support can be daunting, but it's not impossible. With perseverance, hard work, and a positive attitude, you can overcome the challenges and build a successful business. Remember that the journey may be tough, but the rewards of entrepreneurship can be life-changing.

Feeling More Alone

The night was young, so I decided to go to a restaurant by myself. I sat alone at a table in the corner of the restaurant, staring down at my food. I had come here hoping to enjoy a nice meal, but now I found myself feeling more alone than ever. As I sat there, I couldn't help but notice a family at a nearby table. The father was laughing and joking with his two young children, making silly faces and telling them stories. The children's faces were lit up with joy and wonder, and the father seemed to be enjoying every moment of it. I felt alone and felt a pang of jealousy as I watched the other family. I wished I could be that kind of father, the one who made his children's faces light up with joy. But I knew that I had never been that kind of father, and it was too late to change now. I watched as the family finished their meal and got up to leave. I was at my table and felt a sense of sadness wash over me as I realized that I would never have those kinds of memories with my own children. I would never see their faces light up with joy like that. As the family walked past my table, I couldn't help but feel a sense of envy. I wanted what they had. I wanted to be the kind of father who made a difference in his children's lives. But it was too late now. I had missed my chance, and all I could do was sit alone at this restaurant, watching other families make memories that I would never have.

I was sitting at the bar, nursing my drink and staring off into space. The noise of the bar surrounded me, but I barely noticed it. All I could think about were my boys. It'd been weeks since I talked to them. I didn't even know where they were at that moment. I tried calling and texting, but they never answered. I was starting to feel like I lost them forever. I took another sip of my drink, feeling the alcohol numb my senses. I knew I shouldn't be drinking alone like this, but I couldn't help it. It's the only way to forget, even if just for a little while. I thought back to the last time I saw my boys. They were so happy and full of life. I remembered the way they smiled and laughed, and how they always wanted to be around me. But then something changed. I don't know what it was, but suddenly they didn't want to be with me anymore. I took another sip of my drink, feeling the weight of my sadness pressing down on me. I wished I could just talk to them, to find out what's going on. But I didn't even know where to start. As I sat there, lost in my thoughts, I suddenly felt a hand on my shoulder. I turned to see a friendly face, someone I talked to a few times at the bar.

Anthony Gomez

They asked if I was okay, and I started to tell them about my boys. To my surprise, they listened. They offered words of comfort and understanding, and they even shared their own story of loss and heartbreak. For the first time in weeks, I felt like someone understood what I was going through. As the night wore on, I found myself feeling a little bit better. I knew that I still had a long way to go, but talking to someone had helped. I finished my drink and headed home, feeling a little bit less alone than I did before.

In the realm of life's adversities, few experiences can be as emotionally challenging and disheartening as navigating the intricacies of the child support system. For individuals like yourself, who find themselves caught in the crossfire, it can often feel as if you are being treated more like a prosecutor of your own punishment rather than a father who deeply cares for their children. The journey through the child support system can be riddled with frustration, confusion, and a sense of injustice. It is a system designed to ensure the financial well-being of children, but sometimes it fails to acknowledge the complexities and nuances surrounding the dissolution of a marriage or partnership. As you reflect upon your own experiences, it is natural to question the fairness of the system and wonder why it often feels like a punishment. It's important to remember that the child support process is not a reflection of your worth as a parent. It is a legal framework put in place to ensure financial stability for your children, and unfortunately, it can sometimes overlook the emotional toll it takes on you. It is essential to separate the circumstances that led to the end of your marriage or relationship from your role as a parent. While it may be tempting to place blame solely on yourself, it is crucial to recognize that relationships are complex and multifaceted. The responsibility for the end of a partnership cannot be solely attributed to one person. In moments of frustration and despair, it is vital to remember that you are not alone. Many others have walked a similar path and faced the same challenges. Seek support from friends, family, or even support groups specifically designed for individuals navigating the child support system. Sharing your experiences and connecting with others who can empathize with your struggles can provide solace and a sense of community. Additionally, it may be helpful to engage with legal professionals who specialize in family law. They can guide you through the intricacies of the child support system, ensuring that your rights are protected and that you are treated fairly. Understanding the legalities and processes involved can help alleviate some of the frustration and confusion you may be experiencing. Remember, being a father is not defined solely by financial contributions. Your love, care, and presence in your children's lives are invaluable. While the child support system may sometimes feel like a burden or a punishment, it does not define your worth as a father. Stay committed to your children, seek support, and remember that you are more than the challenges you face.

CHAPTER 5

The Beginning of a Deadbeat Father

I was single, and it was a typical Friday night, and I decided to hit up the local bar to grab a drink. The night was young. As I walked in, I spotted a girl sitting at the bar, sipping on her drink. I couldn't help but notice how stunning she looked with her wavy hair and deep brown eyes.

I made my way toward the bar and ordered my drink. As I waited for my order, I couldn't help but sneak a few glances at her. Suddenly, she turned toward me and caught me staring. I immediately looked away, feeling embarrassed. A few moments later, she tapped my shoulder and said, "Hey, I noticed you were looking at me. Do you want to chat?" I was taken aback by her boldness, but I couldn't resist her charm. We started talking, and I found out that she was a college student studying psychology. We talked about our interests and hobbies, and I was surprised to find out that we had a lot in common. As the night went on, we laughed and joked around, and the chemistry between us was undeniable. We exchanged numbers and made plans to meet up again.

As I was reaching for my phone, I noticed a missed call. It was my son calling again. As soon as I heard my son's voice on the other end of the line, I felt a wave of relief and joy wash over me. We talked for hours, catching up on everything that had happened in our lives since we last spoke. I listened intently as my son told me about his new school, his new friends, and the activities he had been involved in. I could hear the happiness and excitement in my son's voice, and it made my heart swell with pride. As we talked, I realized just how much I had missed my son. I felt a sense of connection and closeness with him that I had not felt in a long time. The months we had spent apart seemed to melt away as we talked and laughed together, leaving that female waiting and feeling uncertainty. When the call finally ended, I felt a sense of contentment and happiness that I had not felt in a long time. I knew that no matter how much time passed between our visits, I would always cherish the moments we shared together. And so my son and I continued to talk and stay in touch, building a bond that would last a lifetime. Hearing my son's voice on the phone for the first time after months was a moment I would never forget.

System Harassment toward Fathers

Fathers who are subjected to child support harassment face a daunting challenge of trying to provide for their children while also dealing with the financial burden of mandatory payments. While child support is meant to ensure that children receive adequate care, it can also be a source of immense stress and frustration for fathers who are struggling to make ends meet. One of the main issues with child support is that it often fails to take into account the financial situation of the fathers who are required to pay it. Many fathers are forced to pay an amount that is far beyond their means, leaving them struggling to pay their bills and provide for themselves and their children. This can create a vicious cycle of debt and financial hardship, as fathers struggle to keep up with their payments while also trying to make ends meet. In some cases, fathers may even be forced to take on additional jobs or work longer hours just to keep up with their child support obligations.

Another issue with child support harassment is that it can create a toxic relationship between fathers and their ex-partners. When fathers feel like they are being unfairly targeted by child support enforcement agencies, they may become resentful and bitter toward their ex-partners, which can make it difficult for them to co-parent effectively. This can be particularly damaging for children, who may be caught in the middle of a bitter and acrimonious dispute between their parents. When fathers feel like they are being unfairly targeted by child support enforcement agencies, they may be less likely to want to cooperate with their ex-partners on issues related to their children, which can create additional stress and tension in an already difficult situation. Ultimately, child support harassment only makes things worse for fathers who are trying to provide for their children. Instead of helping to ensure that children receive adequate care, it can create financial hardship and emotional distress for fathers, which can be damaging for both them and their children. To address this issue, we need to take a more compassionate and holistic approach to child support, one that takes into account the financial situation of fathers and their ability to pay. Only then can we ensure that children receive the care and support they need, while also ensuring that fathers are not unfairly targeted or harassed.

My First Paycheck After Child Support

As I opened my paycheck, I knew that this week was going to be a little different. After months of legal battles and court hearings, my child support payments had been finalized, and my salary was now being garnished to pay for my child's expenses. I felt a mix of emotions as I looked at the amount on my paycheck. On the one hand, I was relieved that the legal process was finally over, and I could move on with my life. But on the other hand, I was frustrated that a significant portion of my hard-earned money was being taken away from me. As I sat down to pay my bills, I realized that the child support payments were going to make a significant dent in my budget. I had to cut back on some of the things I enjoyed, like eating out or going to the movies, to make ends meet. But as I thought about my child, I knew that these sacrifices were worth it. But is it when you want to buy food for your kids when they visit you? I wanted to make sure that my child had everything they needed to grow up healthy and happy, even if it meant sacrificing some of my own luxuries. But how can I support myself and my kids if they take a significant portion of my hard-earned money? As the weeks went by, I began to adjust to my new financial situation. I found ways to save money, like cooking more meals at home or carpooling to work. And even though I couldn't afford to do everything I wanted, I found joy in spending time with my child and creating memories that we would both cherish. Looking back on that first paycheck after child support fees, I realize that it was a turning point in my life. It made me reevaluate my priorities and reminded me of the importance of family and responsibility. And even though it wasn't easy, I knew that I was doing the right thing for my child, and that was all that mattered.

CHAPTER 6

Spending Quality Time

As soon as I stepped out of my office building, I knew I had to do something to shake off the stress of the day. And what better way to do that than by taking my son to the park? I rushed home, changed into something more comfortable, and grabbed my son's hand, eager to spend some quality time with him. As we walked toward the park, my son chattered excitedly about his day at school. He was so full of energy, and I couldn't help but smile at his enthusiasm. When we arrived at the park, my son ran toward the playground, eager to climb and swing and slide. I watched him for a few moments, feeling proud of the little boy he was becoming. But I knew I couldn't just sit on the bench and watch him play. I had to be a part of it too. So I joined him on the playground, climbing up the ladder and sliding down the slide with him. We laughed and screamed and played together, forgetting about everything else for those few moments. As the sun began to set, we walked over to the grassy area of the park and played catch with a Frisbee. My son's eyes lit up with joy every time he caught the Frisbee, and I couldn't help but feel grateful for this moment. As we walked back home, my son talked nonstop about the fun we had at the park. And even though I was exhausted, I felt a sense of fulfillment and happiness that only comes from spending quality time with your child. I knew that no matter how stressful work could be, I could always count on my son to remind me of what's truly important—family and fun.

Financial Hardship

There are many causes of child support abuse, including financial hardship, resentment toward the custodial parent, and lack of empathy for the children. Some noncustodial parents may also see child support as a way to control the custodial parent or punish them for ending the relationship. Children who are victims of child support abuse may suffer from poverty, hunger, and lack of access to basic necessities like health care and education. They may also experience emotional trauma, feeling abandoned or unloved by the noncustodial parent. This can lead to long-term mental health problems, including anxiety and depression. Custodial parents who are victims of child support abuse may struggle to make ends meet, leading to financial instability, job loss, and even homelessness. They may also suffer from emotional distress, feeling overwhelmed and unsupported in their role as a single parent. There are legal and social responses to child support abuse, including court orders, wage garnishment, and the involvement of child support enforcement agencies. However, these responses are often inadequate, and many custodial parents continue to struggle with child support abuse. Social responses, such as education and awareness campaigns, can also be effective in addressing the issue. The future of child support abuse depends on the collective efforts of society to address the issue. This includes a greater emphasis on education and awareness, as well as stronger legal and social responses to child support abuse. Ultimately, the goal should be to ensure that all children receive the financial support they need to thrive and succeed. Child support abuse is a hidden scourge that affects millions of children and families around the world. By raising awareness of the issue and taking action to address it, we can ensure that all children receive the support they need to lead healthy, happy, and successful lives.

Child support is a legal obligation that requires noncustodial parents to provide financial assistance for the upbringing of their children. The knowledge of life in child support lifestyles of noncustodial parents is important to understand the challenges and struggles faced by these parents who are required to pay child support. Noncustodial parents who pay child support often experience financial stress due to the high cost of living and the added burden of child support payments. They may struggle to make ends meet, pay bills, and provide for their own basic needs. This can lead to a lower quality of life, increased financial instability, and even poverty. In addition to the financial strain, noncustodial parents may also feel a sense of loss and disconnection from their children. They may struggle to maintain a relationship with their children due to distance, limited visitation, or other factors. This can lead to feelings of isolation, loneliness, and depression. Noncustodial parents may also face social stigma and negative stereotypes, which can make it difficult to find employment, housing, and other resources. This can further exacerbate their financial and emotional struggles. Overall, the knowledge of life in child support lifestyles for noncustodial parents highlights the need for greater support and understanding for these parents. This includes financial assistance, access to resources and services, and greater recognition of the important role that noncustodial parents play in the lives of their children.

A Nonprofit Organization

A nonprofit organization for child support for noncustodial parents who are struggling emotionally could provide a range of support services to help these parents cope with the challenges of paying child support and maintaining a relationship with their children. Here are some potential plans for such an organization:

1. Counseling and emotional support: The organization could provide counseling services and emotional support to noncustodial parents who are struggling with feelings of loss, disconnection, and depression. This could include individual and group counseling sessions, as well as online support groups and forums.

2. Legal assistance: The organization could offer legal assistance to noncustodial parents who are facing challenges with their child support payments, such as unfair or inaccurate calculations, or difficulty modifying support orders. This could involve providing information, referrals, and even pro bono legal representation.

3. Financial assistance: The organization could offer financial assistance to noncustodial parents who are struggling to make their child support payments due to financial hardship. This could involve providing grants, loans, or emergency funds to help these parents meet their obligations and avoid falling into arrears.

4. Parenting education and support: The organization could provide parenting education and support to noncustodial parents, helping them to develop positive relationships with their children and maintain regular contact even when they are not living together. This could include workshops, seminars, and online resources.

5. Advocacy and awareness-raising: The organization could advocate for the rights and needs of noncustodial parents, raising awareness of the challenges they face and advocating for policies and programs that support their well-being and the well-being of their children.

Overall, a nonprofit organization for child support for noncustodial parents who are struggling emotionally could provide a valuable service to this often-overlooked population, helping to improve their mental health, financial stability, and overall well-being.

Child Support Abuse

There are many causes of child support abuse, including financial hardship, resentment toward the custodial parent, and lack of empathy for the children. Some noncustodial parents may also see child support as a way to control the custodial parent or punish them for ending the relationship. As a single mother of two young children, Sarah had always struggled to make ends meet. She worked long hours at a minimum-wage job, but it was never enough to cover all of the bills and expenses that came with raising a family. When Sarah and her ex-husband divorced, she was awarded full custody of their children. As part of the divorce settlement, her ex-husband was ordered to pay child support to help with the costs of raising their children. At first, her ex-husband made the payments on time and in full. But as time went on, he started to miss payments or pay only a portion of what he owed. Sarah tried to talk to him about it, but he would always make excuses or blame her for his financial struggles. As the missed payments piled up, Sarah found herself struggling even more to provide for her children. She had to cut back on expenses and work even more hours to make up for the shortfall. Eventually, Sarah decided to take legal action against her ex-husband to enforce the child support order. But the process was long and complicated, and it took several months before she finally received the money she was owed. The impact of the child support abuse on Sarah was devastating. She was constantly stressed about money and worried about how she would provide for her children. She had to rely on family and friends for help, and it was a constant struggle to make ends meet.

In addition to the financial strain, Sarah also struggled emotionally. She felt betrayed by her ex-husband and angry that he wasn't fulfilling his responsibilities as a parent. She also felt guilty for putting her children through the stress and uncertainty of the situation. Child support abuse is a serious issue that can have a profound impact on custodial parents and their children. It can cause financial hardship and emotional distress and strain relationships between parents and their children. It's important for parents to fulfill their obligations and for the legal system to enforce child support orders to ensure that children receive the support they need to thrive. Child support abuse can also have a significant impact on noncustodial parents. Noncustodial parents are typically ordered to pay child support to help cover the costs of raising their children, but when the custodial parent abuses the child support system, it can cause financial and emotional strain on the noncustodial parent. One of the most significant impacts of child support abuse on noncustodial parents is financial strain. If the custodial parent is not using the child support payments for the intended purpose of supporting the child, the noncustodial parent may be left struggling to make ends meet. The noncustodial parent may have to cut back on expenses or take on additional work to make up for the lost funds. Child support abuse can also cause emotional distress for noncustodial parents. They may feel frustrated and powerless if they believe the custodial parent is not using the child support payments appropriately. They may feel like they are being punished for something they did not do, and this can lead to resentment toward the custodial parent and the legal system. In some cases, child support abuse can also strain relationships between noncustodial parents and their children. If the noncustodial parent is struggling financially because of child support abuse, they may not be able to provide the same level of support and care for their children as they would like. This can lead to feelings of guilt and inadequacy, and it can strain the parent-child relationship.

Overall, child support abuse can have a significant impact on noncustodial parents. It can cause financial strain and emotional distress and strain relationships with their children. It's important for the legal system to take child support abuse seriously and to enforce child support orders to ensure that both custodial and noncustodial parents are fulfilling their obligations to support their children.

A Father's Dilemma

Mark had always been a responsible father. After his divorce, he had made sure to provide for his two children, Emily and Alex. He paid his child support on time every month, and he was always there for his kids whenever they needed him. However, things were about to change. One day, Mark received a letter from his ex-wife's lawyer. The letter stated that his ex-wife was demanding an increase in child support payments. Mark was shocked. He had just received a promotion at work, and he was barely making ends meet as it was. Mark tried to reason with his ex-wife, but she was adamant. She threatened to take him to court if he didn't comply with her demands. Mark was left with no choice but to hire a lawyer and fight the case. The court case dragged on for months, and Mark's legal fees kept piling up. He had to borrow money from friends and family just to make ends meet. Meanwhile, his ex-wife was living a lavish lifestyle with her new husband, who was a successful businessman. Mark's lawyer advised him to settle the case out of court, but Mark refused. He was determined to fight for his rights as a father. He had always been there for his children, and he wasn't going to let his ex-wife take advantage of him. The court finally reached a verdict. Mark's child support payments were increased, and he was ordered to pay his ex-wife's legal fees. Mark was devastated. He had lost everything he had worked so hard for. Mark's life spiraled out of control. He lost his job, his house, and his self-respect. He was forced to move in with his parents, who were struggling to make ends meet themselves. Mark's relationship with his children suffered, as he was unable to provide for them the way he used to.

One day, Mark received a call from his ex-wife's lawyer. The lawyer informed him that his ex-wife had been arrested for embezzlement. She had been using the child support payments to fund her lavish lifestyle, and she had been caught. Mark was shocked. He couldn't believe that his ex-wife had been capable of such deceit. He felt vindicated, but he also felt a sense of loss. He had lost years of his life fighting for his rights as a father, and he had lost his relationship with his children in the process. Mark's ex-wife was sentenced to prison, and Mark was awarded custody of his children. He was finally able to provide for them the way he had always wanted to. However, the scars of the past remained, and Mark knew that he would never be able to forget the pain that he had endured. Mark's story is a cautionary tale about the dangers of child support abuse. It is a reminder that fathers have rights too and that they should be protected by the law. Mark's struggle may have been long and difficult, but in the end, he was able to overcome it and become the father he had always wanted to be.

Child support financial statements are a crucial tool in ensuring that noncustodial parents are meeting their financial obligations toward their children. These statements detail the amount of child support that has been paid, the amount that is owed, and any arrears that have accumulated. One issue that has been observed with child support financial statements is the occurrence of overpayments by noncustodial parents. Overpayments can occur due to a variety of reasons, such as incorrect calculations, changes in income, or changes in custody arrangements. In some cases, noncustodial parents may also intentionally overpay in an attempt to reduce their arrears or to gain favor with the custodial parent. The problem with overpayments is that they can cause financial hardship for the noncustodial parent. Overpayments can result in a reduction in disposable income, which can impact the noncustodial parent's ability to provide for themselves and meet their own financial obligations. Additionally, overpayments can create a sense of resentment and frustration toward the child support system, which can make it difficult for noncustodial parents to maintain a positive relationship with their children. It is important that child support financial statements are reviewed regularly to ensure that overpayments are identified and rectified as soon as possible. Custodial parents and noncustodial parents should work together to ensure that child support payments are accurate and fair and that any overpayments are addressed promptly. In cases where overpayments have occurred, noncustodial parents should be reimbursed promptly to avoid any undue financial hardship. Overall, child support financial statements are an essential tool in ensuring that noncustodial parents meet their financial obligations toward their children. However, it is important that these statements are reviewed regularly to identify and rectify any overpayments that may occur. By working together, custodial parents and noncustodial parents can ensure that child support payments are fair and accurate and that the best interests of the children are always put first.

Family History

Sophie is a curious ten-year-old girl who has always been fascinated with her family history. She has a loving mother and grandparents who have always been there for her, but Sophie can't help but wonder about her father, whom she has never met. Sophie's mother has always been evasive when it comes to talking about her father. All Sophie knows is that her father left before she was born, and her mother has never shared any details about him or their relationship. Determined to find out more, Sophie starts to investigate on her own. She begins by asking her mother more questions, but her mother still refuses to talk about it. Sophie then turns to her grandparents, who are more willing to share some details. Sophie discovers that her father was a musician who played in a band and traveled around the country. He met her mother at a concert, and they fell in love. However, things didn't work out between them, and he left before Sophie was born. Sophie is now more determined than ever to find her father. She starts doing research online and discovers that her father's band still plays in some local bars. Sophie convinces her grandparents to take her to one of the shows, and she finally sees her father for the first time. Sophie is nervous but excited to finally meet her father. She approaches him after the show and introduces herself. Her father is surprised but happy to see her. They talk for a while, and Sophie learns more about him and his life. Sophie's father is now living in another state, but he promises to keep in touch with her. Sophie is overjoyed to finally know her father and has a newfound appreciation for her family history. She realizes that sometimes, the answers we seek are right in front of us, but we just need to have the courage to ask the right questions.

Asking the right questions can lead to finding your answer. Just like Sophie, she didn't care about the situation; she just wanted to know her father's background. In this story, the father sang a song about finding his daughter and all the years he missed her. He expressed his gratitude in front of the crowd emotionally and physically; the crowd responded positively and respectfully. Sophie didn't think for a second about the negative impact that he left her. Slowly she began to approach the stage, and without hesitation, the father noticed and began to speak to her with a song. The band, recognizing the off-tone, began to go with it. All Sophie ever wanted is to meet her father and learn more about the roots between the bloodline she is under. A father's love is the most important part in a child's lifestyle. We speak life into our kids' lives.

John had always been a successful businessman, but his personal life was a different story. He had been married twice and had three children, but he had never been able to maintain a stable relationship with any of them. He was always too busy with work and never made enough time for his family. One day, John received a phone call from his eldest daughter, Emily. She was getting married and wanted her father to walk her down the aisle. John was surprised but thrilled to hear from her. He had not spoken to Emily in years, and he knew he had a lot of catching up to do. John flew to Emily's city and spent a week with her and her fiancé, Daniel. During that time, John realized how much he had missed out on. He saw how happy Emily was with Daniel and how much she had accomplished in her life. He also saw how much he had hurt her by not being there for her. John knew he had to make things right. He decided to stay in the city and work remotely so he could spend more time with Emily and help her plan the wedding. As they spent more time together, John saw how much his daughter had grown and how much she had accomplished despite his absence. John also saw how much he had missed out on. He realized that he had been so focused on work that he had missed out on the most important thing in life—his family. He knew he had to change that. On the day of the wedding, John walked Emily down the aisle. As they walked, John felt a sense of pride and love that he had never felt before. He realized that he had been given a second chance to be a father and to show his daughter how much he loved her. After the wedding, John decided to move to the city permanently. He started a new business that allowed him to work from home and spend more time with his family. He also started to build a relationship with his other two children, and he made sure to never let work get in the way of his family again. John's life had changed completely, and he had finally found what he had been missing—a father's love.

The Impact of Child Support Abuse on Children

Children who are victims of child support abuse may suffer from poverty, hunger, and lack of access to basic necessities like health care and education. They may also experience emotional trauma, feeling abandoned or unloved by the noncustodial parent. This can lead to long-term mental health problems, including anxiety and depression. Child support abuse can have a significant impact on children, both financially and emotionally. Child support is meant to provide children with the financial support they need to live a stable and healthy life, but when it is abused, children can suffer in several ways.

Financial Impact

Child support abuse can cause financial hardship for children. When noncustodial parents fail to pay child support, it can leave the custodial parent struggling to provide for the child's basic needs, such as food, clothing, and shelter. This can lead to instability in the child's life, which can have long-term effects on their development and well-being.

Emotional Impact

Child support abuse can also have emotional consequences for children. Children may feel abandoned or neglected by the noncustodial parent who fails to provide financial support. This can lead to feelings of anger, resentment, and low self-esteem. Children may also feel like they are a burden on the custodial parent, which can cause them to withdraw emotionally. In addition, child support abuse can create conflict between parents, which can negatively impact children. Children may feel caught in the middle of their parents' disputes, which can cause them to feel stressed and anxious. They may also feel like they have to choose between their parents, which can be emotionally traumatic. Overall, child support abuse can have a significant impact on children's financial stability and emotional well-being. It is important for parents to prioritize their children's needs and work together to provide them with the support they need to thrive. Tell yourself this: when was the last time you sat down and had a conversation with your child? Did he/she think that everything is there?

CHAPTER 7

Custody Battle

I am not playing the role of a family attorney. This is what I was told when I was going through my divorce and custody battle. Locate your local attorney for more details. The impact on a custody battle during divorce proceedings can vary depending on different factors such as the state laws, the circumstances of the divorce, and the best interests of the child. Some factors that can impact a custody battle include the following:

As a full-time dad and full-time worker, life for Alex was always a juggling act. He would wake up early, pack his daughter's lunch, drop her off at school, and then head to work. His job as a software engineer was demanding, and he often worked long hours to meet deadlines. But no matter how busy he was at work, he always made time for his daughter. After work, Alex would pick up his daughter from school and take her to her ballet class or soccer practice. He loved watching her dance and play, and he was always there to cheer her on. When they got home, Alex would help his daughter with her homework, cook dinner, and then tuck her into bed. Despite the challenges of being a full-time dad and full-time worker, Alex wouldn't have it any other way. He cherished the time he spent with his daughter and was grateful for the stability and security that his job provided. But one day, everything changed. Alex's company was acquired by a larger firm, and he was told that his job was being eliminated. He was devastated. He didn't know how he was going to provide for his daughter without a steady income. For weeks, Alex searched for a new job, but nothing seemed to be working out. He was starting to lose hope when he received a call from the school principal. They were looking for a new after-school program coordinator and thought that Alex would be a perfect fit. Alex was hesitant at first. He had never worked in education before, and he wasn't sure if he could handle the responsibility. But after thinking it over, he realized that this was an opportunity to spend more time with his daughter while still earning a steady income. Alex took the job, and it turned out to be the best decision he ever made. He loved working with the kids and helping them learn and grow. And he was able to pick up his daughter from school every day and spend more quality time with her.

Life as a full-time dad and full-time worker was still a juggling act, but Alex had found a way to make it work. He was grateful for the challenges and the opportunities that had led him to where he was today, and he knew that he would always cherish the time he spent with his daughter. The story with Alex and his daughter tells the story of what 4% of fathers must do to keep their rights as a father. Sometimes fathers play the victim of "Why me?" when we see a forty-hour check after waging taking out. You must ask yourself, are you willing to be a parent?

1. Primary caregiver: The parent who has been the primary caregiver of the child may have an advantage in the custody battle.
2. Child's preference: Depending on the age of the child, their preference may be taken into consideration by the court.
3. Parent's ability to provide: The parent's ability to provide for the child's physical, emotional, and educational needs may also be considered.
4. History of abuse: If one parent has a history of abuse or neglect, it may impact their chances of gaining custody.
5. Parent's mental health: The mental health of both parents may be evaluated to determine their ability to care for the child.

In some cases, the court may order a custody evaluation to be conducted by a mental health professional to determine the best interests of the child. The evaluation may include interviews with both parents, the child, and other individuals involved in the child's life.

Ultimately, the decision of custody is made by the court based on what is in the best interests of the child. During a custody battle, the parent's ability to provide physical and emotional support for the child is an important factor that the court considers. Physical support includes providing the child with a safe and stable home environment, adequate food, clothing, and medical care, and meeting the child's basic needs. Emotional support includes providing the child with love, attention, emotional stability, and a healthy relationship with both parents.

The court may evaluate each parent's ability to provide physical and emotional support for the child by considering various factors such as their financial resources, work schedule, living arrangements, parenting skills, and mental health. The court may also consider any evidence of neglect, abuse, or substance abuse by either parent. If one parent has a stronger ability to provide physical and emotional support for the child, they may have a better chance of being awarded custody. However, in some cases, the court may order joint custody, where both parents share physical and legal custody of the child. It is important for both parents to present evidence of their ability to provide physical and emotional support for the child during a custody battle. This may include presenting evidence of their financial stability, living arrangements, parenting skills, and any other factors that demonstrate their ability to provide a safe and stable environment for the child. The end of a relationship can be a challenging and emotional time for everyone involved. However, when children are involved, the situation becomes even more complex. Co-parenting is the process of working together with your former partner to raise your children in a healthy and positive environment. It can be difficult, but it is essential for the sake of your children's well-being. In this book, we will discuss the importance of co-parenting and provide some tips on how to do it effectively.

Co-Parenting

Children are the innocent victims of a relationship breakdown. They may feel confused, sad, or angry about the situation; and it is essential to minimize the impact of the separation on them. Co-parenting is crucial because it allows both parents to remain involved in their children's lives and provide them with a stable and secure environment. It also helps to ensure that the children's emotional needs are met and they receive the love and support they need to grow into happy and healthy adults.

Effective co-parenting involves communication, cooperation, and compromise. It can be challenging to put aside your differences and work together, but it is essential for your children's well-being. Here are some tips on how to co-parent effectively:

1. Put your children first: The most important aspect of co-parenting is to put your children's needs first. This means setting aside your personal feelings toward your former partner and focusing on what is best for your children. It is essential to remember that your children need both parents in their lives, and they should not be used as pawns in any disputes.

2. Communicate effectively: Effective communication is key to successful co-parenting. It is important to establish clear lines of communication with your former partner and keep each other informed about your children's well-being. This could include regular phone calls, emails, or face-to-face meetings to discuss any issues that arise. It is also important to be respectful and courteous in your communication, even if you do not agree with your former partner's point of view.

3. Cooperate and compromise: Cooperation and compromise are essential for successful co-parenting. It is important to work together to create a parenting plan that meets the needs of your children and takes into account both parents' schedules and commitments. This may involve making compromises and being flexible to ensure that both parents have an equal role in their children's lives. It is also important to be respectful of each other's parenting styles and decisions.

4. Be consistent: Consistency is crucial in co-parenting. Children thrive on routine and stability, and it is essential to maintain consistency in their lives, even if they are splitting their time between two households. This could include maintaining consistent rules and expectations, discipline, and daily routines. Consistency helps to provide children with a sense of security and stability.

5. Encourage a positive relationship with the other parent: Encouraging a positive relationship between your children and their other parents is essential. This means avoiding negative comments or behavior toward your former partner in front of your children and encouraging them to spend time with their other parents. It is also important to respect their relationship with their other parents and not interfere or try to control it.

6. Seek professional help if necessary: If co-parenting becomes too difficult or complicated, it may be necessary to seek professional help. This could include counseling or mediation to help resolve any disputes or conflicts and find a way forward that is in the best interests of your children.

In conclusion, co-parenting is essential for the well-being of children whose parents have separated. It involves effective communication, cooperation, and compromise to create a stable and positive environment for children to grow and thrive. By putting the needs of their children first, parents can work together to provide the love and support their children need to become happy and healthy adults. If co-parenting becomes too challenging, it is important to seek professional help to find a way forward that is in the best interests of everyone involved.

Legal Obligation

Child support is a legal obligation that is imposed on parents who have separated or divorced, to provide financial support for their children. The purpose of child support is to ensure that the child's basic needs, such as food, clothing, education, and health care, are met. Child support is a legal requirement, and failure to pay it can result in serious consequences for the noncustodial parent. One of the most significant consequences of not paying child support is the loss of rights that the noncustodial parent may experience. In some cases, nonpayment of child support can result in the loss of parental rights altogether. This means that the noncustodial parent may no longer have any say in the child's upbringing and may not be allowed to see or spend time with the child. The loss of parental rights is a severe consequence of not paying child support, and it can have a profound impact on both the parent and the child. For the parent, it can be devastating to lose the right to be involved in their child's life. For the child, it can be equally devastating to lose contact with a parent whom they love and care about. The loss of parental rights is not automatic, and it is not the first step taken by the courts when a parent fails to pay child support. Before a parent's rights are terminated, the court will typically take several steps to try to enforce child support payments. These steps may include wage garnishment, seizure of assets, and even jail time for the noncustodial parent.

The court's primary concern is always the best interests of the child. If the noncustodial parent is not paying child support, then the court may see this as a failure to meet the child's basic needs. In such cases, the court may take steps to protect the child, including the termination of parental rights. The loss of parental rights is not a decision that the court takes lightly. Before making such a decision, the court will consider a range of factors, including the child's age, the relationship between the parent and the child, and the reasons for the nonpayment of child support. The court will also consider whether terminating parental rights is in the best interests of the child. In some cases, the noncustodial parent may voluntarily relinquish their parental rights. This may happen if the parent feels that they are unable to meet their financial obligations or if they feel that they are not able to provide the child with the care and support that they need. In such cases, the court will typically require the noncustodial parent to sign a legal document relinquishing their parental rights. The loss of parental rights is a serious consequence of not paying child support. It is a decision that should not be taken lightly, and it is important for parents to understand the consequences of their actions. If a parent is struggling to meet their child support obligations, then they should seek legal advice and support to help them through this difficult time.

In conclusion, child support is a legal obligation that must be taken seriously. Failure to pay child support can result in serious consequences, including the loss of parental rights. The court's primary concern is always the best interests of the child, and if a noncustodial parent is not meeting their financial obligations, then the court may take steps to protect the child. It is important for parents to understand the consequences of not paying child support and to seek legal advice and support if they are struggling to meet their obligations. Ultimately, the well-being of the child should always be the top priority.

Potential Plans

Reuniting fathers with their children and helping them build a positive relationship can be a challenging but rewarding endeavor. Here are some potential plans for how to approach this goal:

1. Education and resources: Providing education and resources to fathers can be an important first step in helping them reunite with their children. This could include information on legal rights and responsibilities, parenting skills, and strategies for building a positive relationship with their children.
2. Mediation and counseling: Mediation and counseling can be valuable tools for helping fathers and their children work through any conflicts or issues that may be preventing them from being together. This could involve family counseling, mediation sessions, or other forms of support that help fathers and their children communicate and build trust.
3. Support groups: Support groups can be a valuable resource for fathers who are struggling to reunite with their children. These groups can provide a safe and supportive space for fathers to share their experiences, connect with others who are going through similar challenges, and gain encouragement and inspiration.
4. Legal assistance: In some cases, fathers may need legal assistance to help them reunite with their children. This could involve assistance with child custody and visitation arrangements or help with navigating the legal system to resolve any legal barriers to reunification.
5. Community outreach and education: Community outreach and education can be an important part of helping fathers reunite with their children. This could involve working with community organizations, schools, and other groups to raise awareness of the importance of father-child relationships and to provide resources and support to fathers who are struggling to connect with their children.

Overall, helping fathers reunite with their children and build a positive relationship requires a multifaceted approach that addresses legal, emotional, and practical challenges. By providing education, resources, counseling, and other forms of support, it is possible to help fathers overcome these barriers and build a meaningful relationship with their children.

The Isolation of Misunderstanding

As I embarked on my journey through the labyrinthine world of the child support system, I found myself feeling alone and misunderstood. Friends and family, although well-meaning, struggled to comprehend the complexities of my situation. I yearned for a resource that could guide me and provide a clear understanding of the child support system, assuring me that I was not a deadbeat father. This book, born out of my own search for answers, is dedicated to those who have felt the same isolation and confusion. I delve into the intricacies of the child support system, breaking down its components and processes. Drawing from my personal experiences and extensive research, I provide a comprehensive overview of how child support is determined, calculated, and enforced. By demystifying this often-opaque system, I aim to empower readers with the knowledge and understanding they need to navigate their own circumstances. I confront the damaging stereotype of the deadbeat father head-on. I share my own story and those of other fathers who have been unjustly labeled, shedding light on the systemic biases and misconceptions that perpetuate this harmful narrative. Through personal anecdotes and research, I challenge readers to question societal assumptions and recognize the importance of dispelling stereotypes surrounding non-custodial parents. Navigating the child support system can take a toll on one's emotional well-being. In this chapter, I delve into the emotional challenges faced by fathers who have been bullied by the system. By sharing my own struggles and those of others, I provide validation and support for readers who have experienced similar emotions. Moreover, I offer practical strategies for coping with stress, maintaining mental health, and finding a support network during these trying times. I explore the power of advocacy and the importance of empowering oneself within the child support system. Drawing from my own journey as an advocate, I provide readers with tools and resources to assert their rights, seek legal assistance, and connect with support networks. By sharing success stories and practical advice, I aim to inspire readers to become active participants in their own child support battles. One of the most significant impacts of the child support system is often financial strain. As I conclude this book, I want to assure readers that they are not alone in their struggles. By sharing my own experiences, knowledge, and research, I hope to provide a roadmap for change within the child support system. Together, we can challenge the stereotypes, fight for fair treatment, and create a more equitable environment for all non-custodial parents. This book is for those who have felt misunderstood, providing them with the knowledge and empowerment they need to move forward with confidence and resilience.

Printed in the USA
CPSIA information can be obtained
at www.ICGtesting.com
CBHW030756261123
2074CB00039B/46